◆ HISTORY FROM PHOTO

School

Kath Cox and Pat Hughes

Wayland

• HISTORY FROM PHOTOGRAPHS •

Notes for Parents and Teachers

This book provides a flexible teaching resource for Early Years history. Two levels of text are given – a simple version and a more advanced and extended level. The book can be used for:

♦ Early stage readers at Key Stage 1
♦ Older readers needing differentiated text
♦ Non-readers who can use the photographs
♦ Extending skills of reading non-fiction
♦ Adults reading aloud to provide a model for non-fiction reading

By comparing photographs from the past and the present, children are able to develop skills of observation, ask questions and discuss ideas. They should begin by identifying the familiar in the modern photographs before moving on to the photographs from the past. The aim is to encourage children to make 'now' and 'then' comparisons.

The use of old photographs not only provides an exciting primary resource for history but, used alongside the modern photographs, aids the discussion of the development of photography. Modern photographs in black and white are included to encourage children to look more closely at the photographs and avoid seeing the past as 'black and white'. All the historical photographs were taken beyond the living memory of children and most have been selected from the Edwardian period between 1900–1920. A comprehensive information section for teachers, parents and other adults on pages 29–31 gives details of each of the old photographs, where known, and suggests points to explore and questions to ask children.

Editors: Vanessa Cummins and Katrina Maitland Smith
Designer: Michael Leaman
Picture researcher and photostylist: Zoë Hargreaves
Production Controller: Nancy Pitcher
Consultant: Suzanne Wenman

Front cover pictures: The main picture shows an 'object lesson' in a classroom in the early 1900s. The inset photograph shows a parent helping children with their classwork in a modern classroom.
Endpapers: Photographers at work at a wedding, 1907.
Title page: Boys' drill, Leeds, c.1900.

Picture Acknowledgements
The publishers would like to thank the following for allowing their pictures to be used in this book: Beamish, The North of England Open Air Museum **main cover picture**, 15; Chapel Studios **inset cover picture**; Eye Ubiquitous 26 (A.J.G.Bell); Chris Fairclough 8; Hulton Deutsch Collection 21, 27; Leeds City Council Libraries title page, 7, 9; Popperfoto 11; Public Record Office of Northern Ireland 5; Reflections 24 (Jennie Woodcock); The Royal Photographic Society, Bath, endpapers (Stanley Nicholls), contents page, 19 (John Warburg), 25 (Horace Nicholls); Tony Stone 6 (Barry Lewis), 10 (Pascal Crapet); Topham 23; By courtesy of NMS/The Scottish Ethnological Archive 13, 17 (Lothian Regional Council Department of Education); Wayland 4, 12, 14, 16, 18, 20, 22. All artwork is by Barbara Loftus.

First published in 1995 by Wayland (Publishers) Limited
61 Western Road, Hove, East Sussex BN3 1JD, England

© Copyright 1995 Wayland (Publishers)Limited

The right of Kath Cox and Pat Hughes to be identified as the authors of this work has been asserted in accordance with the Copyright, Designs and Patents Act 1988.

British Library Cataloguing in Publication Data
Cox, Kath
School. – (History from Photographs Series)
I. Title II. Hughes, Pat III. Series
371.009

ISBN 0-7502-1540-2

Typeset in the UK by Michael Leaman Design Partnership
Printed and bound in Great Britain by B.P.C. Paulton Books Ltd

·Contents·

A Brownie box camera and case, 1900.

Some of the more difficult words appear in the text in **bold**.
These words are explained in the picture glossary on page 28.
The pictures will help you to understand the entries more easily.

This is a class photograph.

Pupils at this school wear a **uniform**.
The sweatshirts have the name of the school on the front.
The photographer has asked the children to smile.
Everyone looks happy.

This is a school photograph.

Children did not wear a school uniform.
They wore their best clothes to have their photograph taken.
Everyone had to stand or sit still for almost three minutes
while the photograph was taken.

The children are having a school assembly.

This school assembly is in the hall.
The children are sitting on the floor.
The headteacher tells a story and the children say a prayer.
Sometimes they sing a song at the end of assembly.

Schools had an assembly on most days.

Pupils had to stand in silence in the hall.
They were not allowed to sit down.
The children said prayers and sang hymns.
This hall was also a classroom.

The children in this classroom are working in groups.

The **furniture** in the room can be moved around.
Pupils can sit together and talk about their work.
They move around the classroom to collect what they need.
Groups do different work.

Children sat in rows and worked in silence.

They sat on **benches** with wooden **desks** fixed to the floor.
Pupils were not allowed to move around the classroom
without the teacher's permission.
Everyone did exactly the same work.

Sarah is working at her table.

She has lots of different coloured pens, which are easy to use.
Sarah will throw away the felt-tip pens when the **ink** runs out.

Older pupils wrote with a pen and ink.

The pen holder had a metal **nib** on the end, which was dipped into ink.
It was hard to write neatly because the ink made **blots** on the paper.
Younger children learnt to write on **slates** with slate pencils.
Good handwriting was very important.

Miss Lipscomb is a teacher.

Most people go to university or college to learn how to teach.
Many women teachers are married.

Most teachers
learnt to teach
in school.

They worked
as pupil teachers.
After four years
they had to take
an exam.
Few teachers went
to training colleges.
Women had to stop
teaching when they
got married.

These schoolchildren have playtime every morning.

The **playground** is marked out with games.
The children can play or talk to their friends.
A teacher watches the children to make sure they are safe.

Children had playtime in the morning and the afternoon.

Most schools had somewhere for the children to play.
In some city schools the playground was on top of the school building.
Pupils sang songs and played games in the playground.

These children have a hot school dinner.

They choose what they want to eat from a **menu**.
The assistants serve the food.
Pupils sit at tables to eat their school dinner.
Some children bring a packed lunch to school.

The first hot school dinners were given to poor children.

There was no choice of food.
Pupils sat at long tables and their meals were brought to them.
Most children brought food to eat or went home for their dinner.
Some had nothing at all to eat.

Ann, John and Jenny are drawing pictures.

Sometimes they write stories about their pictures
by choosing what they want to say.
Their teacher then writes it down for them.

Children had to copy pictures and writing.

The teacher drew pictures and wrote sentences on the **blackboard**. Then the pupils copied them carefully into their books.

These pupils are having a PE lesson.

They are using special benches and mats in the school hall.
Some children wear special clothes for PE.
Children learn games, gymnastics and dance.
Boys and girls do PE together.

Children had drill lessons at school.

The teacher shouted instructions for the children to follow.

Everyone did the same exercises together.

Pupils wore their school clothes for drill.

Boys and girls were taught drill in separate classes.

Mrs Reed and Mrs Hill are helping the children to make biscuits.

Boys and girls learn how to cook.
In this school parents work in the classrooms with the teachers.

Some children had cooking lessons.

Only girls were taught to cook.

Boys learnt woodwork.

Parents were not allowed to help teachers in school.

Amir is winning a race on Sports Day.

There are lots of different races
on Sports Day.
Boys and girls take part together.
Many families come to watch the children.

Some schools had a Sports Day.

The children wore their school uniform.
Boys and girls ran in separate races.
Parents did not usually go to Sports Day.

Class 5 are on a school trip.

They are visiting a slate mine.
The trip is part of their school project about materials.
They will draw pictures and write about what they have learnt
when they get back to school.

Children went on school outings.

They travelled into the countryside or to the seaside.
Most trips were not part of their school work
but were special treats for the children.

· Picture Glossary ·

assembly When all the pupils in the school come together, usually to sing songs and say a prayer.

ink The coloured liquid that is inside a pen, used for writing.

benches Long seats made of wood.

menu A list of different meals to choose from.

blackboard A large board painted black and written on with chalk.

nib The metal point of a pen.

blots Spots of ink on paper.

playground A place for children to play.

desks Pieces of furniture. A desk has a flat or sloping top to rest on for writing.

slates Slate is a kind of stone. It was split into thin flat sheets called slates for children to write on.

furniture Tables, chairs and other things that can be moved around in a room.

uniform Special clothes that are the same style and colour and are worn by all the pupils at a school.

·Books to Read·

At School by K. Bryant-Mole (History from Objects series, Wayland, 1994).
At School by G. Tanner and T. Wood (History Mysteries series, A & C Black, 1992).
Our Schools by S. Ross (Starting History series, Wayland, 1992).
School Day by M. Stopplemann (Turn of the Century series, A & C Black, 1990).
Victorian Children by A. Steel (Beginning History series, Wayland, 1989).
A Victorian School by R. Wood (Victorian Life series, Wayland, 1993).

·Places to Visit·

Many local museums have collections about schools in history so it is worth contacting them to see what they can offer. Those listed below have a reconstruction of a Victorian classroom.

History of Education Centre
East London Street
Edinburgh EH7 4BW

    Telephone: 0131 556 4224

Ragged School Museum
48 Copperfield Road
London E3 4RR

    Telephone: 0181 980 6405

Museum of Childhood
Judge's Lodging Museum
Lancaster
Lancashire LA1 1YS

    Telephone: 01524 32808

Beamish
North of England Open Air Museum
Beamish
County Durham DH9 0RG

    Telephone: 01207 231811

Ulster Folk and Transport Museum
153 Bangor Road
Cultra Manor
Holywood
County Down
Northern Ireland BT18 0EU

    Telephone: 01232 428428

Welsh Folk Museum
St. Fagans
Cardiff
South Glamorgan CF5 6XB

    Telephone: 01222 569441

· Further Information about the Photographs ·

School photograph, 1903.

About this photograph
By 1900 the school leaving-age was 12 years. Most pupils attended their local board Elementary school. From 1902 Britain had a national system of free education for pupils under 12. There are many examples of school and class photographs from this time. Few children look happy – partly the result of having to keep still for so long while the photograph was being taken. Having your photograph taken was a new and rather solemn occasion. The school photographs were not produced to be purchased by pupils (as today) but as a record for the school.

Questions to ask
What is happening in this photograph?
Why is no one smiling?

Points to explore
People – number, age, gender, appearance, pose, clothing.

School assembly, a Leeds Board school, c.1900.

About this photograph
Assemblies were a regular part of school life and were religious and moral in tone. They were regarded as very important. A special assembly took place at the end of the year. Prizes of books or certificates were given to pupils who had done well or attended regularly.

Questions to ask
What is happening in this photograph?
Who are the adults in the room?
Why are there desks in the room?

Points to explore
People – number, age, gender, clothes, pose.
Background – room-size, furniture, lighting, features, decoration.

Infant class, a Leeds Board school, c. 1900.

About this photograph
By 1901 there were over 4.5 million children attending Elementary school. The school leaving-age was 12 although a few pupils stayed on until they were 14. The emphasis was on the three 'Rs' and pupils were expected to pass the 'Standards' of reading, writing and arithmetic. Classes were large and discipline was strict, even with the youngest pupils.

Questions to ask
What are the children doing?
What equipment are they using?
Why are the desks so close together?
What differences are there between this classroom and yours?

Points to explore
People – number, age, gender, appearance, clothing, pose.
Classroom – design, layout, furniture, equipment, lighting, decoration.

Boy writing, c.1900.

About this photograph
This is a posed photograph probably taken in a photographer's studio, not a classroom. Younger children began by writing with their fingers in sand trays. They moved on to writing on slates with a special pencil so that mistakes could be erased. Once they could form letters correctly, pupils were taught to write with pen and ink. A child would be ink monitor – to ensure ink wells were kept full. Much time in school was spent perfecting handwriting.

Questions to ask
Where was the picture taken?
Who might the boy be?
What is on the top of the desk?

Points to explore
Boy – age, pose, appearance, clothing.
Background – furniture, equipment.

A teacher, 1911.

About this photograph
Training for Elementary school teachers required only a period as a pupil teacher (varying between two and five years). This involved 'brighter' pupils staying on at school and working as the teacher's helper. Some were able to finance a college course after two years in order to qualify. Women teachers were forced to resign if they got married. There are examples of women concealing marriages, husbands and children from the school authorities in order to keep their jobs.

Questions to ask
What is the woman holding? Why?
What is she wearing on a chain around her neck?
Why did she have her photograph taken?

Points to explore
Teacher – gender, age, appearance, pose, clothes.

Outdoor play, Hunstanworth School, Co. Durham, 1910.

About this photograph
The school day generally ran from 9 a.m. to 4.30 p.m. with two ten-minute playtimes and a two-hour lunch break (to allow pupils to go home for dinner). The passive nature of learning for all including the youngest pupils meant that children needed the period of physical activity provided by playtime. Some of the traditional playground games, such as hopscotch and singing rhymes, are still played today.

Questions to ask
What kind of area was this school in?
What different activities can be seen?

Points to explore
People – number, age, gender, clothes, activities.
Background – buildings and their features, materials, scenery.

PHOTOGRAPH ON PAGE 17

Dinner time at North Canongate School, c.1914.

About this photograph
School dinners were a recent introduction and were provided by only a few schools. This innovation reflected concern about children's health. A sample menu might be soup followed by a pudding. This cost a penny but the very poorest children received free dinners. Most school children brought a frugal lunch, such as cold tea and bread, or went home.

Questions to ask
Why are there so many adults in the room?
What are the children eating?
Why are some children not wearing shoes?

Points to explore
People – number, age, gender, clothing, activities.
Hall – size, layout, furniture, lighting.

PHOTOGRAPH ON PAGE 19

Children drawing, c. 1910.

About this photograph
Schools placed great emphasis on rote learning and copying. Creativity was rarely encouraged in children. In addition, teachers had few visual aids or textbooks to use. Therefore, they wrote information on the board and children copied it down or memorized it. Art lessons were rare and consisted of children copying patterns.

Questions to ask
Where was the photograph taken?
What might the children be drawing?
What are they drawing with?
How do you think the children feel?

Points to explore
People – age, gender, clothes, pose.
Technology – colour photography (this is an autochrome).

PHOTOGRAPH ON PAGE 21

Girls' drill lesson, Townsend Road School, 1905.

About this photograph
Drill lessons were based on army exercises. They were first introduced for boys as a way of instilling discipline in pupils and improving their fitness. Lessons were gradually introduced into the timetable for girls as well. However, the sexes were usually taught separately. Drill usually took place outside school but, on very cold days, the children stayed in the classroom.

Questions to ask
Where was the photograph taken?
What are the girls wearing?
What else is this room used for?

Points to explore
People –age, gender, appearance, pose, activities.
Background – building features, materials.

PHOTOGRAPH ON PAGE 23

Girls' cookery lesson, c.1910.

About this photograph
Much of girls' education focused on preparing them to be wives and mothers soon after leaving school. Concern over the declining standards of housewifery and motherhood in the first years of the twentieth century led to lessons in cookery, laundrywork or sewing being introduced for girls at Elementary schools. Lessons for the boys could include woodwork, drawing (technical) or gardening.

Questions to ask
What different activities can you see?
What kinds of cooking equipment are the girls using?
What is the adult doing?
Why did only girls have cooking lessons?

Points to explore
People – age, gender, appearance, pose, activities.
Background – furniture, lighting.

PHOTOGRAPH ON PAGE 25

School Sports Day, 1912.

About this photograph
Few schools had their own sports fields. From the uniform worn by these girls, this school looks to be a more affluent institution. For most pupils, Sports Day would be a fairly informal experience. A more significant event was the annual Field Day organized by the Sunday Schools. This was usually held on a Saturday in a local farmer's field. Children raced for prizes such as books and pencils.

Questions to ask
Do the girls know the photograph is being taken?
What is the lady in the hat doing?
Would it be easy to run races wearing a school uniform like this?

Points to explore
People – ages, gender, clothing, activities, pose.
Background – buildings, scenery, time of year.

PHOTOGRAPH ON PAGE 27

Norton Road County School. Fieldwork, 1913: a geology lesson on Icknield Way.

About this photograph
Outings or fieldwork were not usually a regular part of the school timetable. Some schools did organize a special outing in the summer for pupils (and often parents, too). However, children were more likely to have this experience through the local church.

Questions to ask
Did the people know the photograph was being taken?
Why was it taken?
What might the children be looking at?
What might be in the rucksack that the boy in the foreground has on his back?

Points to explore
People – number, age gender, pose, appearance, clothes, activities.
Background – area, time of year.

· Index ·

(Items that appear in text)

32